1 9 8 7

BOOKS AND CHAPBOOKS BY A. POULIN, JR.

POETRY

In Advent: Poems, 1972.

Catawba: Omens, Prayers & Songs, 1977.

The Widow's Taboo: Poems After the Catawba, 1977.

The Nameless Garden, 1978.

The Slaughter of Pigs, 1981.

A Nest of Sonnets, 1986.

A Momentary Order: Poems, 1987.

TRANSLATION

Duino Elegies and the Sonnets to Orpheus (Rainer Maria Rilke), 1977.

Saltimbanques (French Prose Poems by Rainer Maria Rilke), 1978.

The Roses & the Windows (French Sequences by Rainer Maria Rilke),
1979.

Poems (French Poems by Anne Hébert), 1980.

The Astonishment of Origins (French Sequences by Rainer Maria Rilke),
1982.

Orchards (A Sequence of French Poems by Rainer Maria Rilke), 1982.

The Migration of Powers (French Poems by Rainer Maria Rilke), 1984.

The Complete French Poems of Rainer Maria Rilke, 1986.

Anne Hébert: Selected Poems, 1987.

ANTHOLOGIES

The American Folk Scene: Dimensions of the Folksong Revival
Co-Editor with David A. DeTurk, 1967.

Contemporary American Poetry First Edition, 1971; Second Edition, 1975;
Third Edition, 1980; Fourth Edition, 1985.

A Ballet for the Ear: Interviews, Essays, and Reviews by John Logan, 1983.

A MOMENTARY ORDER

Poems by A. Poulin, Jr.

For Thoms Mailer —

with best wishes

and gratitude for the request

Al Poulin

1/5/93

GRAYWOLF PRESS, 1987

ISBN 0-915308-92-4

Library of Congress Catalog Number 87-80009

2 4 6 8 9 7 5 3

First Printing 1987

Publication of this volume is made possible
in part through generous donations to
Graywolf Press from the National Endowment for the Arts,
corporations, foundations and individuals.

Graywolf Press is a member organization
of United Arts, Saint Paul, Minnesota.

Published by G R A Y W O L F P R E S S

Post Office Box 75006

Saint Paul, Minnesota 55175

Grateful acknowledgment is made to the editors of the following journals in which some of the poems in this book (or earlier versions of them) were first published:

The American Poetry Review: "Elegy"; *Chicago Review:* "The Singers"; *Choice:* "Prisoners" and the ninth section of "The Slaughter of Pigs"; *Denver Quarterly:* "Calco di Cadevere di Donna: Pompeii," "A Nest of Sonnets," "Saltimbanques" and "September 1, 1979"; *The Journal of Popular Culture:* "Buddha and the Pirates"; *The Kenyon Review* (Second Series): "A Momentary Order"; *Mid-American Review:* "Daughter's Song," "Factory Hands" and "Poem on a Photograph of a Young Painter"; *New American Review:* "The Front Parlor"; *New England Review / Bread Loaf Quarterly:* "Husbands and Lovers"; *New Directions:* "Begin Again"; *New Letters:* "Children in Fog"; *The North American Review:* "On Our Unborn Child" and sections 1, 2, 4, and 5 of "In Advent"; *The Ohio Review:* "The Slaughter of Pigs"; *Poetry Now:* "Geese" and "Moon-Rocks"; *raccoon:* "The Dance of Mimes"; *Salmagundi:* "Figures in a Stranger's Dream," "Lament in Spring" and "Song in Spring"; *The South Carolina Review:* "Shadows"; *Tar River Poetry:* "In the Sleep of Fathers" and "The Wait"; and *Thunder Mountain Review:* "Makers and Lovers."

The inscription for "Saltimbanques" is from the novel *Cora* by Daphne Athas (The Viking Press, 1978) and is reprinted with the permission of the author.

The inscription for "White Sound: Letter to Robin Morgan" is from a poem by Robin Morgan entitled "White Sound" (*Depth Perception,* Doubleday & Co., 1982) which was unpublished at the time I read it and is reprinted with the permission of the author.

The version of "Geese" in this collection originally appeared in *The Congressional Record* (June 13, 1978), as read by the Honorable Silvio Conte (D) of Massachusetts as a tribute to Ada and Archibald MacLeish.

"The Slaughter of Pigs" was also issued as a pamphlet by *The Ohio Review* in 1981.

"The Front Parlor," "To My Brother," "To My Aunt," "To My Sister," "On Our Unborn Child," "In Advent," "To Daphne on the Third and Fourth Days of Her Life" and "Buddha and the Pirates" were originally collected in *In Advent: Poems,* E. P. Dutton & Co., 1972.

"Geese," "The Nameless Garden" and "Prisoners" were originally collected in *The Nameless Garden,* Croissant & Co., 1978. Special thanks to Duane Schneider.

"A Nest of Sonnets" was issued as a separate pamphlet, *A Nest of Sonnets,* by BOA Editions, Ltd., 1985.

Several poems in this book originally bore individual dedications which I've decided not to reprint here for a variety of reasons. Those dedications, however, have not been erased entirely. You know who you are.

I am grateful to the State University of New York, College at Brockport, for sabbaticals, to The Research Foundation of the State University of New York, to the Literature Program of the National Endowment for the Arts and to The New York Foundation for the Arts for fellowships in poetry, and to the Corporation and Staff of Yaddo for residencies during which most of these poems were completed.

—A. POULIN, JR.

CONTENTS

III.   *A Momentary Order*

❦   ❦   ❦

for

BASILIKE *and* DAPHNE

I

IN ADVENT:
FIGURES IN
A STRANGER'S
DREAM

The Front Parlor

Whenever someone in our family
died, the wake was in our house,
downstairs, in the front parlor.

It was a spare room, really, and,
except for a few extra folding chairs,
empty and unheated. The shades were

always drawn, the best lace curtains
hung. And in that constant cool
twilight, the wallpaper damp

as banks of carnations, when we
dared to go in, forbidden to,
we played like shadows under

the great cross, the enormous
suffering, dying or dead Christ,
the room's only constant ornament.

It never was a living room.

•   •   •

I've slept above the dead before,
my bed in the same far corner
as their caskets. Assured their lips

were sewn, their arms clamped,
I've fallen asleep to the rhythm
of hummed rosaries. My grandfather,

choosing to die on New Year's day.
His wife, big-boned and stubborn,
paralyzed for fifteen years,

bedridden five, decaying three,
gangrene growing on her back
like some warm carnivorous herb.

An uncle who never spoke a word
until the week he died, insane,
babbling the poison of his liver.

          •   •   •

I've slept above the dead enough.
Whole generations of a tribe. Still,
in the middle of the night, I hear

the prayers of the living and the dead,
a crescendo through the floorboards,
filling my room like an ancestral chorus:

Que les âmes des défunts reposent
en paix par la miséricorde
de Dieu. They have burned

the seams of their eyes, chewed
the nylon cord threaded through
their lips. They have cast off

their clamps. They stand at my
bedside every night moaning my name
off endless strings of beads, burning.

She plants a growing kiss on my forehead.
With her green hand, moist as moss,
wide as my skull and, forever free,

she strokes my back and thigh.

To My Brother

You'd think there was no end to this
tribe. They set out and multiplied
as if survival of their species

depended on the acid of their sperm.
Now, in the middle of the night,
they call us to come bury their dead.

So we make that black pilgrimage
back to Lisbon to slide one more
familiar corpse into the holy hillside.

We've buried twelve of them, a dozen
deaths survived, with still a dozen more
or so to live through. The horror

of their deaths and lives lives on
and haunts us: Mandia bent and stunted
by that monster riding her shoulder,

lied into believing she was partly angel;
Blackie drunk before his couple suns
rose every morning of his life, except

the last; and Larry loving various wives,
not one of them his own, his children
strangers to him even when he hemorrhaged;

one Émile lingering for months in
hospital beds infested with leukemia's
piranha, another dropping on the corner

during lunch-hour, gaping blindly back
at the mill hands watching our father
take him in his arms and whisper the act

of contrition to his soulless head.
Time and time again I resurrect them.
They gather in my head, eat, drink and

sing, celebrating their own wakes,
prolonging our interminable deaths.
But each time I return from burying one

of them, all the way back home from
Lisbon I can feel unremembered and
unknown parts of me vanish in the dark

and exhausted silence behind me.
They die, Normand, they die.
And, dying, they kill our only history.

❦   ❦   ❦

To My Aunt

All through your life
    they lied to you. They said
        a baby sitter dropped you

and never told your
    mother. They never could
        admit that you were crippled,

born deformed, your shoulder
    jutting out into the blade
        of a stunted wing. Therefore,

they said, you could never
    lead a normal life, and,
        therefore, you never did.

The mutant of our crippled
    wills and hearts, you played
        tribal nurse and clown,

the fool of our cruelty and needs.
    I don't think you ever knew.
        Today we buried you.

No. You were even spared.
    that simple fact: ice sealed
        the ground, a clenched and final

pack of lies. But you
    are dead, and, dead, leave
        me obsessed by that hump

and bright lie on your back.
            After they pronounced you
                        dead, drained your blood

out of your veins and dressed
            you like a helpless child,
                        was it impossible for them

to close that cage? Did
            your arms, furious, push back
                        the leaded lid? Did they raise

you, then, turn you over
            and with a hammer gently
                        crack the cartilage of your wing?

Poor dead thing,
            we should have told you all
                        along that you were only partly

human. Then, perhaps,
            neither girl nor angel,
                        that one thrust of yours

bandaged by your skin,
            with its invisible burning
                        mate, might have grown, grown

larger than your frame.
            Before we'd had a chance
                        to break that wild wish

riding on your back,
            you could have winged
                        yourself away from our lies.

Instead, what you were
        and always will be, now
                always will be trapped

inside the mausoleum
        of our fabricated memory
                until they bury all of us.

But tonight, before
        the ground has thawed, before
                they stuff you in its mouth

rigid as an owl
        at dawn, let me open up
                your cage; let me touch

both sides of your wounded
        back; let me heal you.
                Oh, with the new moon

cracking on the snow
        and all your sisters
                chained to their dying

husbands, sleeping,
        let me show you now
                the truth about yourself.

Just once, *believe*
        the light you feel
                trembling behind you.

Let that inhuman
power carry you. *Do
it. Try. Slowly now,*

*easy. Rise, yes.
More. Oh, yes. Now
hover. Soar. Fly! Fly!*

❦   ❦   ❦

In the Sleep of Fathers

A mist rose from the river and hovered
in the air, a heavy slab of granite.
Tongues of satin ribbons flapped *Father,*

Father, Husband, Brother from the wreaths
and baskets of dyed flowers on the rented
artificial turf, while your casket quivered

on the tiny elevator that goes down for-
ever. An ancient woman watering her rock
garden in the rain, the priest sprinkled

holy water over you and intoned that last
incantation for the dead's longer lasting
life, for the deeper sleep of fathers.

The night before, when all your relatives
and friends had left, your sons and daughters
lingered in the mortuary with our mother.

We plucked flowers from the bank that rose
around your bier, a mad farmer's garden
cultivated on the face of some slate cliff,

and lay them as ourselves on your steady
chest, in your hands already grafted
to your ribs. My brother held you in his

outstretched arms, the son he never had,
and begged you to be born again, while we
held each other as we never would again.

Then it was over. Your brothers, sisters,
friends walked back to their cars and slowly
drove off through the cemetery ruled by

our family name. Our wives flanked our mother.
And the undertaker pulled back that blanket
of damp roses children buy to warm their dead.

My brother and I broke two sprigs of ever-
green and placed them just above your mouth.
We knelt and kissed your sealed, implacable

pod one last time. With our knees and feet
still wet with that rich earth surrounding
you as you root yourself deeper, sturdier

in this ground we walk on, in our dreams
we tend to our own families. No longer
sons, we work, we sleep in the sleep of fathers.

❦   ❦   ❦

Prisoners

I wait until my wife and daughter have survived
the hope of nightmares I can never satisfy.
I wait until the quick-freeze traffic of shifts stops
and factory workers weave to work or home as you did,
until the hot screech of tires has turned cold and mute
in two-car garages under sleek and impotent creatures
serene as saints becoming extinct. . . .

I wait until bars close and my students, higher on
nine months of terrifying freedom from their fathers
than on grass, have fallen into one another's arms.

Father, I wait until that blue, blue moment between
pitch night and milk light when I can almost hear you
whistling those melodies you invented for yourself,
that slow time holding light back, back,
when you were alone and slowly drank your coffee
near the hot wood stove in our small kitchen in Lisbon
in winter, as much at peace as you may be now,
because you wanted it that way. I wait. And when
your presence fills this room with that calm
I slept in as a boy, assuring me I am your son
again, I know it's time to go back to your grave.

Your headstone penetrates the half-light of this
granite sky; but it's no wider than a common cot.
I stretch my heavy body over yours until
the ribs' pressure is returned. I could fall asleep
here. Instead, the hands you gave me gently trace
the small and fragile contours of your shoulders
and your hips. And when I've discovered precisely

where you are, I speak to you—those few words
I've unburied for so few, just to bury them again.

The ground begins to heave, slowly; grass tongues
my ear, a language of love no one understands or
wants to. In the mist rising from the brown river, I can
hear the wide white mouths of the many dead I've loved
breathe a single breath that trembles all to silence.
But *Son. I love you. I forgive you your sins.*
are still prisoners inside your mouth.

Before the sun can touch me, before all those workers'
desperate eyes open, traffic begins again and my family
discovers I am gone, before I walk back into their light
—with my body still in the furrow it has ploughed,
I plant the only seed a guilty firstborn son can
sow, Father, to make us live forever.

The Nameless Garden

I built bonfires of brandy
in my mouth and eyes just
to melt the snow falling
on your lips, the forests
of frost rooted in your hazel
eyes under their closed lids.

In every muscle that I have
I erected dykes of whiskey
to dam the water that might
rise out of you or touch you,
touch, then flood you, rampage
each square inch of you.

I froze my brain with gin
to quench the blazing sun
before it burned your small
bald head, before humidity
sucked a thin eternal moss
out of your wide forehead.

Now maples burn, a gold
fire that doesn't consume;
a softer multicolored flame
spurts from the backs and wings
of pheasants in our field where,
safe from hunters, they can mate

near the thin and silent stream
that gradually stops and is
transformed into a brilliant path
of ice back through the woods—
at peace in a necessary sleep—
to an oasis of silence the purest

white, a garden where no creature,
where nothing, ever lives or dies,
a nameless place my own sleeping
genes remember and long for, long.
Father, I've tried to kill myself
for years to save you from your death.

Once again days shorten, darkness
comes more easily and welcomed. If
I could, I would fly back to Lisbon,
mark off the precise dimensions of
your grave, resurrect your coffin,
pry it open with my own bare hands,

press my mouth against your mouth,
my wrists against your wrists, and
give you back your breath and blood.
But I can't survive us both for long.
In the wilderness you've entered never
to return, offer yourself up to water

that will gently wash your bones until
they're clean and white and free of
life, until the blinding framework of
your body *is* that nameless garden where
all streams converge, where frost and sun
are one, and where you and I, my Father,

finally can be together and at peace.

❦   ❦   ❦

Figures in a Stranger's Dream

The day you knew your father would give up
his farm in Canada and pack the nine
kids in a hired car to Maine, where his

seven sons could get jobs in the wool
and cotton mills (maybe work a small farm
on the side), you slipped out your window

late at night and stole down to the pasture
where, over tender mounds of grass in their
green fire, spring's cold moonlight hovered

like the dreamt-of echo of an absent snow.
You tore your nightgown off, let fall your hair
until it flowed, a fountain's shimmering

scrim around you, then, with a dancer's breath-
less leap, you straddled your Pa's old and docile
bull, spurred him with your naked heels and,

in a single ring of light, a sphere of
brilliant, pure, accelerating thrust
that fused your porcelain limbs with that

aging creature's sheer brute bulk, you rode him,
rode and rode him, until dawn broke blood-red
under him, until the bull collapsed, until

your brothers came to lift your wet, exhausted
body off its haunches, wrap you in a blanket,
and carry you back to your bedroom in

a wordless covenant that would almost
outlast your lifetime and our own—
as if you had never lived that night, except

as figures in a stranger's dream.
                              Old woman,
no one's ever known the contours of your
dreams, the figures roaming at their centers.

You spent most your life nursing your father,
as his mouth and eyes filled with greater blank,
and your paralyzed, undying mother,

who fertilized the furrows of her bed
for years with the refuse of her own
decaying flesh until she seemed to root,

a ferocious houseplant feeding on
the breath of unmarried daughters. Breathless
with asthma, nights you spent by your bedroom

window crumbling your beads, novenas
herbicides ravishing your tongue while
more moonlight than your young heart could

absorb and hope to sleep began to flood
the field, foam and fleece and tide, until
the current in the knots of barbed wire

crackled blue, precise and absolute—
even on the night that old woman died,
your name filling her mouth with her last breath.

And you mothered your unmarried brothers
like three farmers' loyal wives: cooking
as many as nine meals a day, cleaning,

hanging their washed underwear and pants
to dry on winter mornings when the cold
snapped at your fingers with the vengeance of

your mother's gangrene. You put them to bed
when they come home drunk after one more night
with the bovine wives of friends and strangers.

And you buried each of them, one by one,
in that overcrowded family plot
where your name was already branded

in a slab of granite. You sold the farm,
equipment, furniture, your brothers'
hand-made tool-chests, mother's linen, crystal

wedding gifts. For days you burned photographs,
love letters, postcards from honeymoons you
never had—anything that would light up the sky.

The last survivor, now the whole history
of the clan, from your great-grandmothers' names
to the glorious fury at the heart of

an unreaped field in moonlight, burgeons
inside their collapsing chests as you live
out your days in a three-room apartment

that shelves on the parish cemetery where
from your bedroom window you can see snow
fall, the disintegrating petals of lost passion.

Tonight your cragged and ancient face is
a worn, familiar planet in slow orbit
above the family pasture where the cattle

of your dreams and mine gently graze a sparser
winter grass. And before your name breaks out,
blooms on the far horizon, obliterates

this small patch of moonlight I cultivate
just by dint of my own breath and hand
as a farmer's son should do, I plumb

a history I have learned, hunch my shoulders,
wish muscles I have never had, flare
my nostrils, call down one last dream of

a young and porcelain woman,

                                        Aurora,

sleepwalking in a scrim of hair,
and offer you my eager, docile back.

To My Sister

All day the dead are still.
Anchored in the hangar
in the hillside, their arms

clamped wings of wild
prehistoric birds
at the bottom of the sea,

they rock, gentle with the tides,
the tilting earth and winds,
invisible and benign.

It's at night, when nothing
living moves, when mirrors
open up like caskets

that they start. Whining,
trembling, the fuel of
their familiar fury burns,

and they sail, horizontal,
moving at inhuman speeds.
Their feet propel them.

The whole armada of our
clan invades my lawn
churning like the sea,

the few fathoms of air
I claim as mine. Huge
and deadly destroyers,

they violate my skull's
sovereignty I've fought for
for years. Anne, tonight

they've come to fight and win.
I feel the infrared blinking
of their eyes in mine. And,

ready to launch the torpedoes
of their hearts, the humming
of their spinning ribs tracks

my heart beat, beat by beat.

The Wait

I've been expecting you
all night. All night
my table's circle of
bright light trembled,
the corners of the room
blasted off into space.
I've been waiting for
you to be there across
from me, finishing some-
thing you'd started to
say so many years ago,
perhaps beginning what
you never could before.

All night I've waited
for you to come from
that other realm, a moth
consummating your mission,
eyes red with an inhuman
fire flashing, flashing
a code it could take me
a lifetime to decipher,
or just to stand there
at the dim edge of my eye,
the fern's fine fronds,
a green shimmer of breath.

Watching me without one
word would be enough.
Because, brother, father,
final lover, all night
I've been expecting you.
Now dawn hammers joists
back into place, blots out
my lamplight. Calm seeps
in. You won't come and,
if you do, I won't be here.

On Our Unborn Child

TO BASILIKE

Cleopatra in the guise
   of Theda Bara plastered
      on our bathroom wall

has immortal longings
   every night about three
      in the morning, and with thick

papery flutters, rustling
   wings on the angel of death,
      collapses in the bathtub.

The Corvair's exhaust pipe
   and muffler have succumbed
      to road salt and to rust,

fallen, and every morning
   as we roar to class,
      monoxcidal fumes ride

the rush of cold air
   from the heater, tempting
      us to sleep and dreams sturdier

than those we've awakened
   from to go to every day,
      every morning, every night.

And poor Jack, the rare
    late autumn days have knit
      his jaw into thick clumps

of orange skin wilting; rot
    blisters on his lower lip;
      a gray moss beards his chin.

A month ago he was our own
    St. Elmo's fire smiling
      two-toothed above the lawn,

as we sailed through another
    year of strangers in this old hulk.
      Tonight the dull fire of his mouth,

hissing as it burns
    the soft pulp of his head,
      might be the foolish glow

of gas above a marsh or graveyard.
    Jack should be in bed,
      his head hollowing a pillow.

Jack looks like my grandmother,
    her face caving in to gangrene
      eating away inside her head

until she died, mouth
    open, an enormous foul hole
      behind her lipless grin.

And me, Love, Christ, look.
    My pores are swollen: beads
      of skin cluster on my chin.

They tell me as I get older
   I look more like my grandmother
      when I smile. Last night I dreamed

she was sleeping beside you.
   She wore Jack's hollow head.
      Love, I dreamt I was dead.

Look, Love, while you bloom,
   the rest of us decay.
      Flies buzz around our eyes.

But I'll have the muffler fixed.
   Tomorrow I'll dispose of poor Jack's head.
      Let the dying bury the dead.

And you, bloom to one
   inside you, one who'll live
      my grandmother's name,

my father's name and mine,
   a child born at Christmas time,
      my seed thriving in you, my slime.

In Advent

FOR BASILIKE AND DAPHNE

I

According to our calculations
You were expected long ago.

But still you crouch inside
The cage of your mother's veins,

A creature conceived by another
Creature, winged, sacred, secret.

Others like you have been known
To be too early or too late

And we've been always unprepared.
Advent is our only season.

2

Although this winter night's
Ablaze with shafts of lightning

Edged with mauve and echoes
With the roar of thunder

Like the sea crashing down
On a pursuing army,

What can I do? I can't
Deliver you from your captivity.

And once you've escaped
Into this wilderness

Where every night promises
No more than itself, and you

Have shown a measure of good
Will and a capacity to survive,

I'll be of no greater use
To you. I'm no one's delegate.

My laws are my own, shifting
With the sand I walk on.

I can't legislate for you, and
I won't promise you the land

When I can't promise you today.
I'm amazed by every morning:

I sing and dance, even for the sand,
And praise the burning at my feet.

Child, I am a desert creature,
One of a nomad tribe, accustomed

To betrayal by the mirage of need.
But this is what I chose,

With David, Ruth and Paul: exile,
The terror of the constant sun

Obliterating every trace of prayer
And law from the ghetto of my tongue;

The wind demolishing my words,
Dust seeping into my bones;

Rats spying on my every wish,
Attacking every hope every night.

But this is what I chose,
Rather than complicity with prelates

Who, with a Nazi zeal,
Will execute their own,

Make candles of their fat,
Thuribles of their skulls,

Stoles of their embroidered skin—
Sacramentals for their rituals

To preserve the sweet, rich blood
Of their infected race.

I am obsessed by the memory
Of murdered friends.

In dreams I finger their bones
Like beads, burning.

Their ashes stir and glow
In the reliquaries of my eyes.

If you choose to search for
Still another atmosphere, Child,

You'll have to find your own
Way out. I can't deliver you.

3

You'd think yours is going to be
Another virgin birth, redemption

In some Iowan farmer's stable,
Cornhusks for your cradle,

Attended by the Aga Khan,
Pope Paul and Martin Luther

King. I see them kneeling,
Wise in the wealth of silos,

Silent, round and solid
As the towers of old temples;

TV antennas, stainless steel
Angels on rooftops transmitting

Heavenly messages to farmhands
Dozing on the frozen hillsides.

4

Where do we go from here?
What frontier, sea or galaxy

Will we have to cross disguised
As night creatures, warming our hands

To the thin embers of twigs,
Feeding on cactus and raw fish,

Slaking our throats with salt
Water or juices of wild locust,

Like fugitives to find asylum?
What drunken governor, anxious

For the safety of his state,
Will sign your execution?

How many children will soldiers
Slaughter so you can live?

In what desert, jungle, city street
Or campus will you wage the war

The rest of us keep losing
Every day? Each day conquered.

What friend will betray you
To the priests? What priest

Will sell you to the state?
Child, we're all Black, all Jews.

Every minute is an exodus.
Hours roar like cattle trains.

Each day is an oven.
Our skulls wish for the bullet's kiss.

How many governors and good
Citizens will be saved by law and order?

Will I live because you died?

5

Child, I don't know
If you've been fathered

To be a prince of peace
Or criminal. My name

In the official census
Is Joseph. All I can

Do is build a bed
And roof for you, supply

You with my name,
My blood and race,

My species; then, season
After season, wait.

DECEMBER 9, 1966

❧ ❧ ❧

To Daphne on the Third and Fourth Days of Her Life

You live and breathe
in a simulated atmosphere,
rarified, behind a shield

of glass, protected
from our infected
air, your natural

habitat. I visit you,
a stranger to your needs,
touch and speak to you

with the help of media:
an intercom and nurse,
sterilized and masked,

disinfected intercessor.
Contaminated, dangerous,
I am still your father.

I'm your originator.
For centuries it seems
I watched you make

your way into my world.
With my ear pressed
against the wall of skin

that separated us,
I heard you swim from side
to side, primeval, precious

fish in my wife's sea.
I later felt the contours
of your spine, the probing

of your foot or fist,
child, still not quite
born, still not quite human

enough to breathe my air.

2

Today I bring you home.
I am prepared to sterilize
utensils, bottles, nipples,

boil the water you will drink.
If needs be, I'll sterilize
the sterilizer, eradicate

a whole race of bacteria
with a Hitler hysteria.
I'll be antiseptic.

But I can't purify
this air you'll breathe.
The air, the air—it is

diseased. It germinates
despair. It can't be
filtered of the shrieks

of burning tongues, throats
melting in Hiroshima,
Auschwitz or in Viet Nam.

Each day and night smells
of dead burnt fat and hair.
Each breath will grease

your lungs, atomic soot
will plug your throat.
What artificial respiration

can I provide for you?
Poems are my iron lungs.
These weird contraptions

pump and pump my chest,
pressure me to survive
each day. I live in

their chambers and praise
the current that makes
them work. But I

can't make a poem
strong enough to help
us both. No poet can

or will. Someday you
may discover or invent
your own machinery

to survive. Until then,
we're still divided
by that wall that separates

the living from the dead.

Buddha and the Pirates

Enshrined in a doorway,
your eyes blue as Ming
chips, you sit cross-legged,
fleshy, round and ringed,
a Buddha bulging
with miraculous paps.
Enameled angels wait
on you, bringing you huge
babies to be nursed, six
at a time, all orphans.
There are so many you can
never satisfy them all.
So, in a slow, deliberate
gesture of beneficence,
you recline on your side,
smile, and grow as many
breasts as your torso can
support, suffer babies
to be brought to you
until you start to tremble,
grace flowing out of you.

Our lawn is a green sea
we sail alone, second-storey
explorers. Defenseless
in our pullman sloop,
we search for coves
and inlets, peninsulas
of our marriage's continent.

We never heard them come.
We never even saw the skull
and crossbones of their black
flag glowing above their sails.

They swing on the masts
of trees, arms flashing
like sabers, and, soaring
on the red wings of sleeves,
their captain lands in our room.

He stokes your hair, his
fingers at home in such fire.
I call him scoundrel, but he
hauls you to himself, a precious
spoil. His mates are laughing,
multicolored in the trees. Gray,
I'm not strong enough to fight
him off and watch the two of you
sail off toward the open sea.

3

Morning sails into our bed-
room, the splintered
ghost of a Venetian ship.
You aren't here. I find
you in the sunlight
of the alcove. Once more,
across the ocean of my
deepest nightmare, you've
come back, our baby at your
breast. Love, my Buddha,
you are always here.

II

MAKERS

AND LOVERS

Narcissus

If I look in the mirror
long, and long enough,
I see myself naked
now for the first time
by a distant silver pond
at the center of a forest
no lover has explored.

Astounded by the miracle
of bones, inhuman symmetry
of muscles, I worship
my torso: the gentle mist
of hair on my legs; the thin
spray rising from my loins,
a shimmering fountain of
down; my arms curved necks
of swans swimming away
from me; my penis arched,
a silent tongue bridging
tenderness and terror;
my neck a mountain water-
fall; my face the fall of lovers.

If I look at myself long
and love enough, I too can
feel the addling fury of joy
that must have seized another
after he'd stared at a flawed
marble pool so long, he saw
a boy, who'd topple giants, flower.

Lament in Spring

At the heart of that thick grove of pines
beyond the lawn, at high noon
today I found a tiny and unearthly-
pale blue egg, more fragile

than an eye, that had fallen from a nest
and floated in a blinding
pool of spring-fed sunlight—the foetus of
a rare and undiscovered

starfish. With my fingers interlaced
into a cautious net, I
slowly scooped it closer to my face
just to wonder at its color,

just to thrill over such a brittle shell.
But when I breathed a deeper
breath of awe, that small egg shattered
in my open palm—and once

again I felt the wing of madness brush
my temple with the fury
brooding in the ova of all fragile
things for centuries. My friend,

in this sometimes gentle world where we must
give and give and give just
to survive, there are things that do and
always will shatter merely

from the brunt of awesome human breath.
We have been two of them.
Tonight, as I prepare for sleep, I stand
before the mirror, shimmering

with its antique silvered weight: my naked
body glows its own pale hue
and once again I am as vulnerable
as any man-made thing.

Stars plummet into distant seas, the wind
gusts, and one tiny feather,
clinging to my thinning hair, wildly flutters
inches from my pale blue eye.

Song in Spring

TO BASILIKE

The lilies of the valley that I picked
for you faded in one day.
But all day those white and tiny bells
poured the breathless music

of their odor in our room and made us
dizzy, as in dance or
as—on a brilliant morning in the Alps
while canton bells intone

the Angelus—lovers who have tasted
death. Tonight their ecstatic
perfume's music echoes still in consort
with Mozart's mild sonatas,

and the crystal vase that was their brilliant
sepulchre for one rare day
is still ringing with so much of their
memory beyond the pitch

of sound, it threatens to disintegrate
into a dust of light
and root itself in our flowerbed.
By morning that vase will be

empty glass again; we will have forgotten
flowers that so briefly graced
our lives among demands of daily love
and work: these words with wills

of steel I labor to anneal into
a tougher tongue; the fired
metal which you forge toward that sound of
a pure language all your own;

this marriage that continues to refuse
to break under the brunt
of habit and assumption. But tonight,
let the dream of these frail, white

lilies speak: Love, if death must touch our tongues
when we are in full bloom,
then let our memory survive that grave
business in our music's wild perfume.

Daughter's Song

Daphne, another day
    of tiny miracles
        as frangible as

daughters in their
    slow, tender blooming
        into strong and lovely

women, ineffable
    epiphanies, revealed
        more by the light

song of their being
    all and only what they
        are than by any telling.

This morning two pale
    mourning doves, like aged
        lovers who have learned

love's longer-lasting
    tongue, coo their
        soft monotone lament,

echoed by the bees
    that pollinate the air
        around this magnolia

with perfume that might
    make younger lovers
        wild with love's anxieties.

In the hemlock near
　　my door, a robin's
　　　　nest, as vulnerable

as any shelter
　　that a father builds.
　　　　In it: four brilliant

eggs asserting those
　　clichés of their blue
　　　　with a loud and brittle

melancholy, as if
　　they were being hatched
　　　　in Eden. On my desk

the mushroom that I
　　picked two days ago:
　　　　withered, dehydrated,

and now the small
　　but labyrinthine
　　　　heart-shaped dead brain

of a unicorn,
　　its horn still and
　　　　forever locked in place,

the tip blossomed
　　into white lips thick
　　　　with a purer pitch of love,

the ecstasy of speech.
　　You see, there are things
　　　　in this often silent human

world a father cannot
        teach his daughter.
                He can only speak them:

Dove. Egg. Mushroom.
        And the fire that I
                built to ward off this

early evening chill
        flares in my eyes again
                as its warm laurel tongues,
                        without song, sing: *Daphne.*

❦   ❦   ❦

Children in Fog

TO M. W.

Ebbtide: a thin fog sails in from the sea
and moors on the Atlantic
coast. Houses vanish, our neighbors on
the beach start to dissolve

and each thin thread of hair on our bodies
turns to white, heavy with
a warm and gentle sea-mist. Suddenly,
we are figures in this land-

scape's dream again, floating in and out
of one another with the heave
of tides and exchanging histories
like breath in lovers' mouths.

In our children's eyes, we are fathers
flying toward the vanished point
of our own history, returning only
in their dreams, as we always

will; and where the sea and the horizon
fuse, they are baby dolphins
leaping out of breakers, stuttering that
music we inhaled, once, long

ago, and hammered into tongues of law.
Neither males nor females of
their species, they still love themselves so much
they are buoyant in this mist,

their wake bright parabolas of light. They swim
toward us so slowly, they could
never reach us in our lifetime or their own.
Michael, they're so substance-

less, they might also dive into our eyes
and nest there deep inside
our brains to resurrect as memories
remembered in another life.

The landscape dreams us into motion;
we dream ourselves leaping from
a brilliant sea; we wake in
an imaginary country,

strangers in these strangers' heavy bodies
white with frost, a music in
our throats as primordial as scrimshaw
replicas of our descendants—

and we drown, only to awaken once
again, here, on the Atlantic
coast, as our children's names soar from our open
mouths until they swim toward us

again and we know they are still safe.
In this haze that has become
as much light as it is water, Michael,
this could be the day when

children of the sea first breathed oxygen
and miraculously walked
on land—or that other, when the offspring
of this earth long for hydrogen

again, unleash its law that will impose
a momentary order
all its own, when, like the other fathers,
we'll come to this coast again

and wait for our bodies' every sinew
to blaze brightly, from within,
for our children's bodies to collapse
around their feet like starfish,

while the music from their vanished mouths
will leap back into the breakers,
back into the throats of dolphins swimming,
slowly swimming in our eyes.

Factory Hands

I

He comes here every day after his eight-
hour shift, his forearms shining with that
deep and lasting glow of good industrial oil.

Wisps of cotton still cling to his hair;
his body's filaments are spun tight spools
of muscle; the bass whine of the spinning

room reverberates in the porous fibers
of his bones. He strips and swims; he swims
the drone of lubricated gears out of his

system for another day. Spent as a husband,
he rises from the sea, glistening with sea
spray and with salt, stretches on the sand,

offers his exhausted body to the sun. He sleeps.
For minutes that could last the lifetime he
will never live, he breathes bright sunlight.

What impossible ambition, what inhuman lover
sprouts a dream inside his lungs, travels
his veins' entangled vineyard, ripples every

tendon into bloom, writhes and arches his
whole body till he softly moans—as if
an unknown tongue of satisfaction touched

his very center once, and then again? Ahh,
this beautiful young man's body will be
wasted with his dreams long before he wakes,

before he's thirty, sullen, married to some
sullen woman in a weave of mutual betrayals
where the automatic murder of each other

or their kids will be the casual nightmare
of their hopes. And the sea's incessant hum
will vibrate in his inner ear, as all that

elaborate machinery of his life, gone berserk
with useless overuse, spins out of control,
and the last few shreds of love, of all desire,

unravel at his feet on a blazing summer after-
noon, in the middle of some eight-hour shift.

2

I've known this sleeping stranger all my life.
He's one of those young men, their eyes as old
with unrelenting terror as their fathers',

I worked with years ago in the wool and cotton
mills to pay my own way out of my father's
futile dreams. He is my younger brother.

Even to this day, he never has forgiven
me: my bone-white, small and delicate hands;
my unmanly fumbling with machinery;

my working hours weaving tapestries
of sound with no more than the thin strands
of my brain; my passion for escape; my will

never to be some factory hand collapsed
in base exhaustion on any blazing beach
or bed. And in the universe of just

reversals, he is me divining this
young stranger's dream of who *I* just might be.

3

I have come here every day after another
sleepless night, my thighs still wet with
the sweat of lovers—faceless, masterful

mechanics of the body's warp and woof,
its every joint and screw. After having
been worked over by those technicians of

the machineries of pleasure, my every
nerve-end aches with memory still spinning
from its center, a residue of ecstasy

that no lye or Atlantic would wash out.
Glistening with the last few drops of
coconut oil some beautiful young thing

bought me in Hawaii, I begin a new
day's work: the plots, the intrigues, rumors
of the grapevine—no less elusive than

the irreversible burst of those small
veins in the blue arbor of my ankles,
the bubbles of bright blood that refused

to burst in the press of my own stubborn
heart. My friend, my beautiful young brother,
this stranger sleeping next to me, never

could fathom why I come here every day
to offer my own oiled, exhausted body
to the sun, to sleep another lifetime,

pray ultra-violet rays of suns
in still another universe to obliterate
the memory of all human and inhuman

lovers, the bloom and seed of uselessly
abused ambition, before the compli-
cated machinations of my life

grind to a halt and, in the middle of
some blazing summer afternoon, un-
ravel in my brain, my mouth, a tongue,

a language, just one simple human phrase
or word—a weapon gone berserk.
My friend, let our beautiful strange brothers sleep.

Poem on a Photograph
of a Young Painter

TO K.E.

You stand before your painting
of a soldier's empty shirt that hovers
vertically between the azure
of a stormed Aegean sky, the flesh tones

of a frail imagined beach.
With one hand in your pocket, your full weight
resting on one leg, you wear
your own brilliant white silk shirt, tinged bronze

by your body's olive hue,
your designer's jacket of soft black velour—
the clothes you wore the last time
that I saw you, at home and comfortable

in the old world splendor
of the Hotel Grande Bretagne in Athens;
but your body has assumed
the same posture as that army tunic

suspended in mid-air
by the relentless memory of a warm
and wounded presence, still shaped
by the absent contours of the young man's

body it discarded on
a long-deserted battlefield no one's
ever won—and now become
the vestment of a dark and terrifying

angel. In your letter's
broken English, you say you must set your
daily art aside and, soon,
report for your years of service in one

of this world's oldest armies.
Now you must learn the tactics of a more
ancient art: to recognize
the enemy that hides even in a lover's

heart and, without honor,
without guilt, but with the calculated,
mindless gestures of that long-
danced liturgy of war, to kill and to be

killed. My friend, don't look for me
in this poem's loosely measured syllables;
for before you have arrived
at that wordless momentary peace all

art offers to another,
I will have stepped outside of this
ballet of breath, climbed a ladder
of my own making back into that

photograph of you, and leapt
into your painting; and there, in mid-air,
between the azure bolt
of hopeless sky and the more familiar

human beach, I'll have assumed
that disembodied shirt as if it had
been mine from the beginning,
and I shall hover over

you, unseen, as if, from one
dimension to another, this warm breath
in your hair tonight were mine,
so that other angel cannot leap from

the fabricated realm of art
and with vengeance clamp its dark vestment
of despair around your all-too-human
body, your all-too-guileless heart.

❦   ❦   ❦

White Sound: Letter to Robin Morgan

There is a poem missing here
like the deliberate flaw the Navaho weaver
leaves in her blanket—to let the soul out.
That poem would be a luxury, a passion;
it could afford trust, it could have something
to do with love. . . .

— ROBIN MORGAN

I've been thinking about men all day, the sound they make
when there's no one around to hear them weaving sounds
around a flaw for their heart's own slow release.

This is the sound the new-born man-child makes as his foreskin
is sliced off for sanitary purposes that will not save his
body or his soul.

This is the sound the adolescent boy makes in his dreams as the
stranger with his father's voice laughs at that useless labia
wrapped around his thing, then hacks it off with his hunt-
ing knife.

This is the sound that young men make when they sit together
drinking, talking on a porch in Saratoga Springs in a lone-
liness that will never be consoled, and suddenly their words
stiffen their own tongues like violent strangers' cocks
inside their mouths.

This is the sound men make when the silence at the sight of
a sudden tenderness in them shrivels up their eyes like
testicles unexpectedly immersed in the cold blue of the
Atlantic.

This is the sound men make when the seeds of some unspeak-
able love in them die in the pit of their own hands and
suddenly burst into flames like sons.

This is the sound men make as they fall into pools of sunlight on the forest floor beneath the weight and worry of the unsung music in the story of Ulysses and Penelope.

This is the sound of one old man, drunk on brandy, as he tap-dances his Step-'n-Fetch routine alone in the moonlight when there's no one near to comfort him at dawn.

This is the sound men make as they vanish in the canvas that they thought they'd filled with their own lives.

This is the sound of men shattering in an intolerable symphony of muscle.

This is the sound men make when, because of mindless pleas-antries of sex or race, their white fists pound brick walls until they're blue, then black, then bloody as a buck nigger's on the rack.

This is the sound of young men in a hundred foreign fields as they collapse beneath the kiss of their stranger brothers' bullets.

This is the sound of men in cubicles and cells, in jails, monas-teries, submarines, as they invent themselves, trace the contours of their bodies with a creator's care, fill each other with the tender hum and power of their very lives, then, like ancient women, lie there as their souls escape through the flaws of their own hearts—with passion, trust, perhaps something to do with love.

This is the sound a boy makes as he's raped by his mother's or his father's lover.

This is the sound men make in their terrifying love of daughters who can never be protected from the sound men make.

This is the sound men make in the threadless maze of their love of women and of one another.

This is the sound of one man, forever in a forest of white sound, falling.

Elegy

After Photographs of Anne Sexton by Arthur Furst

I

In your chapel of butter and daisies,
you sit at a workbench, a pew, a pine
slab polished too often for coffins.
Sunlight pours over half of you: your
right breast heavy with milk turning
sour, fingers darts of white flames—
vigils rising to challenge the sun.

Just above your head, in the shadow,
a narrow flag repeats *Peace* and *Pax*
and *Rahu* and *Sulh,* a nebula of tongues
you never heard, that never touched you.

You have buried your face, your eyes
that dared stare back at god, in your
other hand, your only comfort. And,
sister, mother, lover, you lean toward
a terrible dark. A round gold watch
watches and beats against your heart.

2

Fingers. Your incredible fingers.
Your long and lovely fingers all
aiming at your face. Scalpels,
kitchen knives, stilettos, tongues
of tribes, the buried faces calling
for you rising from convulsions.
Arrows Sebastian longed for so much.

Your white-blue eyes are stopped,
amazing marbles now, soldered in
their sockets. You stared at one
lens too long, too hard. You never
believed in your own power, Medusa.
Now the roll of an eye, crook of a finger. . . .
Your voice's mirror shatters the shutter.

3

White. White. You stand in a white
embossed gown, framed in white.
A sheet forever blank. So much space.
Your watch still against your heart,
you look straight out and smile. Your
eyes and lips have told it all before.

Gold bracelets ring your arm, a diamond
stashed for passage, and your bare elbow
aims at that flight of fixed black
stairs behind. You climbed, up and down.

4

A woman like that isn't a woman, quite,
who'd dazzle Cambridge and bewitch beautiful
boys into lovers drunk on black and white.

A woman like that isn't a woman, quite,
who'd fly over suburbs with angels at night,
ride through town dressed in red or naked,

blowing kisses to the crowds at the stake.
This is the kind of woman who brakes.
No bracelets, rings or make-up, wearing

just a common polka-dot blouse, she's leaning
back against the refrigerator in her kitchen
with its curtains of cotton gingerbread men.

This is the woman before and after the pack,
slumped in satisfaction, smug, about to laugh,
her pad and scrawl out of the picture, hidden

forever. This is the woman on the rack.
This is the woman who gambles the odds.
This is the woman who devours her gods.

Shadows

My shadow sheds its own pure light.
As you come closer, its translucent
shade darkens blue, trembles toward
the shape it needs to be, something
I once was becoming—perfect, free.

My mouth fills with the language
of the spectrum. Sunlight blinds our
backs and thighs. Our eyes soften.

But you never reach the edges of our
hand hovering above the tips of blades.
Light shortens. I can feel myself
fade and vanish in the rustle of grass.
You are the light my shadow sheds.

Moon-Rocks

National Air & Space Museum
Washington, D.C.

What else did we expect they'd find, those first
two astronauts who landed
on the moon, reduced to less than human
scale by the dimension of
the moment that unfolded right before
our eyes huddled by the moon-
glow of television sets in darkened
living rooms? The artifacts
of planetary angels who became
extinct at the moment breath
was first breathed into human blood? Ruins
of another lost world,
Atlantis risen from Pacific tides?
No more, perhaps, than just half
of one crudely chiseled arrowhead?

We already knew the moon
never could sustain life as we know it.
While Mike Collins sailed the lunar
orbit of the mother-craft alone,
Neil Armstrong and Buzz Aldrin
did precisely what they had
been trained to do: walk across the barren
landscape of our dreams, more slowly than we
had remembered, and gather
rocks no bigger than our fists and hearts
shaped by galactic winds.

Locked in a man-made bezel of far
more common substance, each day
now they're on display for old
witnesses and adolescent skeptics
to come see for themselves and,
trembling with regret or scorn, dare to touch
one more small, pale moon-rock worn
smooth by the kiss of a million other
swirled fingertips of pilgrims.

The Dance of Mimes

He plays a pennywhistle & she begins
to dance alone, high above the pale moon

of his melancholy face, her whole frame
swaying, swaying cautiously in rhythm

with the music of his breath, the slow pitch
of this earth revolving on its axis

in a day-long pirouette around the sun.
In the glare of spotlights, her face soon

becomes a brighter & more wistful echo
of her partner's, & her silk sleeves billow

as her arms stretch out into a tightrope
walker's brittle poles of equilibrium

weighted down on either end with nothing
but the heft of bated OOOO's rising

from our open mouths. The music quickens.
Now there's danger in her dance: one sound

too shrill, one excess beat could topple her
& kill her illusion of a dancer

dancing deftly on no more than the beam
of light refracted by our eyes—that dream

of one moment of such pure perfection
we too would risk all just to know it once.

The clown, with his exaggerated tear
drawn beneath his fractured eye, whirls

& whirls around the grounded pivot of his loud
whistle, leaps & prances through the crowd

of upturned faces that ignore his all-
too-human face. Instead, we watch that tall

& transformed woman: her whole body is
a singing tree of motion that's transfixed

in an incarnate gesture of pure speech—
until she's total woman or sheer freak.

Still, while spotlights orbit her fierce eyes
in a slow ballet of planets & while cries

of *bravo* split the music, she just tilts
her gaze to smile & dances wildly on her stilts.

The Singers

With their arms flung over one another's shoulders,
   breasts and backbones resonating as they touch,
      these six young men are sculptured by the music

that they sing. Originating in the solid bar
   of marble that's their ground, a silence surging
      toward the shape of sound, it rises into feet

and ankles, forms and tempers the thick muscles
   in their calves and thighs, accentuates the sloping
      contours of their hips. The wish for music fuses

with the growing hum of breath inside their chests;
   doubles; strains their ribs until they vibrate
      at a breaking point; arcs the taut fibrilla

ringing in their spinal cords, the tendons
   in their necks; and elevates their faces, eyes
      and opened mouths to the pitch of speechless

agonizing joy—until, precisely when the music
   that they are would be transformed into one clear
      reverberating note sustained as long as marble

might endure, it turns upon itself; plunges
   back into their throats; and fills their bodies
      once again until they seem one step removed

from leaping like a line of dancers out of stone;
   until these six young singing men, with the last
      resounding chord of marble's own leap into song,

would come crashing down, a band of Cossacks stamping
    out an affirmation of the loud and wild reverberations
        of utter human presence, aspiration, act.

Such a buckling of muscle, breath, and lust to prove
    that we exist and that in all creation only we can
        choose to be, to nullify our basic chemistry, become

the incarnate reproductions of our tongues'
    stunning entrechats carved in high relief along
        the wall that separates us from brute silence,

stone and static space and thus, like extinct
    hunters, to survive ourselves as we once did
        in the caves of Altimira—the bright imprints

of our hands (around recumbent bison, leaping
    deer and the retreating boar), fired by the phos-
        phorescence of our kind's longing to endure,

still glowing in the limestone of those walls.
    What if those chiseled replicas, somehow, so be-
        lieved in the figure of the human which they imitate,

in the music pulsing in their veins, you'd swear,
    more absolute than plasma and, suddenly transformed
        by such belief and feeling themselves even only

partly human, they did leap out from this slab
    bolted to the wall? The fission of that cloud
        of marble molecules, still clinging to their backs,

into a mass of sheer amazement in their mouths—
    at the very moment they first sensed the earth's
        vibration at their feet—would disintegrate both

them and us into that pool of excess energy,
  disorder's realm beyond most mortal apprehension,
    except as mathematics for physics' formula and law,

but still forever inaccessible and mute.
  For now, in the afternoon's last slant of light
    receding from that room in Saratoga Springs,

the breath of other poets still buzzing in the glass
  about to shatter, while their tongues' fire echoes
    in the beams and smolders like a brother's threat

of bursting into fierce and all-consuming act
  (remembered one year later here on the coast of Maine
    where the brilliant, blue, relentless music of the sea

sculptures the Atlantic shore with an endless
  tide of aspiration for perfection, mirrored
    by the heaving of the earth, and coastal rocks,

resounding with the moon's galactic pulse,
  are intricately massive incarnations of
    the ever-changing arabesques of waves)

perhaps it is enough to focus what remains
  of attention and desire on that smaller,
    somewhat older figure standing in the distance

of a bas relief, his trunk almost invisible
  behind the thick and splaying limbs of that
    raucus calabash of singing fellowship.

He is alone, his eyes, his mouth closed and calm,
  his arms gently crossed in total concentration
    on his breast, as if he were utterly fulfilled

with listening, as if no human or inhuman
  sound outside of him could modulate
  the solid vertical of his serenity,

as if he were about to fly back sound-
  lessly into the very origins of sound,
    as if he would efface himself and us in sound.

ᵚ   ᵚ   ᵚ

Calco di Cadevere di Donna: Pompeii

FOR JOHN LOGAN

I

Lady, I have resurrected this old
   postcard photograph of you while
      rummaging among mementos we accumulate

as proof that we have occupied
   another time and space, perhaps some
      other lifetime, more perfect than this one,

when we were merely tourists in those
   ancient capitals of pain where even
      daily anguish seemed fired to the pitch

of art and we still had faith in beauty
   smoldering at the heart of suffering, needing
      nothing but a glance to flare and suddenly

transform itself from ordinary
   bone, blood and flesh into astounding presence
      and outlast the sound its dying makes.

Lady, I have lived too long and logged
   too many miles on foot to still believe
      this dust that aches my bones and grates my throat

and swirls in fury in my lungs could blaze
   into a beautiful concerto
      and negate the crush of entropy

in every particle of ash of me;
   but your graceful calcified cadaver,
      this cold winter night, rekindles my belief.

II

That is the perfect posture for anguish:
　　your body turned away from it, your face
　　　　buried in your arms, and your enormous

weight balanced on your elbows and your knees;
　　with the gentle slope of your long legs,
　　　　the rise and fall of your small hips and breasts

carved by lava's frenzied hand, Lady,
　　you're more perfectly human than David
　　　　standing naked in Firenze's public square.

A mother trying to protect
　　the petrified foetus inside you,
　　　　you're an ancient lover, too, arched

above the man who's already vanished
　　in the very love of you. Solder for an-
　　　　other mouth, your burning lips kiss nothing

but the space beneath them, frozen into
　　silence, your smooth buttocks raised above
　　　　your belly, knees and naked feet in anti-

cipation of a pleasure, penetration
　　and amazement that may never end—
　　　　that moment of unearthly passion and

anxiety before the barely human
　　touches the divine. In one astounding
　　　　instant that the rest of us must struggle

for a lifetime to achieve, you blazed,
　　bloomed, and became the consummated gesture,
　　　　word, the emblem that few creatures ever

give to others. In your endless seething,
  endless undulation in the agony
    of passion, that grace which is most ours,

the curved and fragile bridge between
  the terrible and tender, you are
    what this earth, in its decreasing orbit

of the sun, returns to survivors
  and to other lovers sometimes: the name-
    less gift of lava rising from its center

like a tongue reaffirming the sublime
  breath brooding one small egg of glorious
    music in each cell of bone, blood, flesh.

III

Snow has begun to fall, a familiar
   welcomed ash; an alarming fire's
      raging on a distant hill; my wife

and daughter have long faded in the dark-
   ness of my breath; and the veins in both
      my legs throb rivulets of molten rock.

While we remain inhabitants of this
   planet still in flux, through the last
      dimension that will always separate us,

before I fall asleep in nostalgia
   for another place, and with only that
      small space beneath you to be filled

before you walk away, a vision
   consummated without act, tonight, *Donna,*
      I want to slip my body under yours.

Makers and Lovers

TO JOCELYN SLOAN

As if a speck of diamond dust had lodged
itself under each eyelid
and gently etched the corneas, I close
my eyes and some creature's

crystalized unearthly shape glitters into
focus in the sunlight pooled
beneath my thinning lid, then swims its slow
insistent gallop down

into the darkened caverns of my brain
and just as slowly canters
long and graceful strokes back to the edge
of light. That creature, Jocelyn,

has been roaming in me since my childhood:
it rode the rapids of my blood,
grazed the green herb garden at the center
of my glowing ribs; in dreams

it reared and then leapt from my brow,
a free, ecstatic totem.
Far from the Atlantic coast, its untamed,
more familiar tides, I sit

on a wide, trim sward beside a swimming
pool: rippled by the wind, sun-
light is a cloud of lunar landscapes
sailing at the pit of this

pale green palm of water, always open
like the artificial eye
of a more luxurious race and age
staring blindly at the sun.
Such transformations make me dizzy.

I am a farmer's first-born
son accustomed to a tougher truth,
a hard-earned, hard-lost vision.
Remembering your love of all that's strong

and beautiful and thrives deep
inside a maker's and a lover's chest,
a hardy cool potato
absorbing minerals from the earth, I close

my eyes to catch that creature's stroking
gallop in the blazing dark
behind my lids again: the hard-working
sea-horse of my name and kind,

bracing moon-hauled tides on his vertical
in a sea of horizontals,
this untameable white beast of beauty's
hunt: the deadly unicorn.

Geese

IN MEMORY OF ADA AND ARCHIBALD MACLEISH

The scalene angle's point pierces the horizon;
light tears. The V widens for miles. Another.
Then another. The sky darkens, the air throbs
under the pound of wings, cracks to the call
of hundreds of them migrating back to Canada.
After a multi-thousand-mile flight over oceans
and mountains and jungles and cities, and, almost
home, these geese soar over the last Great Lake,
as sure of their target as missiles or angels
deployed by gods. Unarmed by the awe that fills
our open mouths season after season, all we can
do is stare.

      We are the unbelievers who have
trod the moon's white dust in disbelief and jet-
tisoned magnetic waves of our voice, the radar
of our heart toward uncharted galaxies to trace
even just one other planet's pulse and prove that
in this cosmos we are not unique—only to return
to earth, the terminus of our trajectory, more
human, more alone.

      Now in the soft tilled loam
of our friend's family garden, as we track today's
last flock of northbound geese, almost invisible
against the darkened sky, we are rooted in a moment
of amazement under arcs of brilliant single sylla-
bles of breath, ignited in our throats and blooming
in the early evening air like exploding rockets
at a local county fair celebrating still another
season's harvest.

Our faces, our hands are
raised by a supplication that starts in our feet
and clings to the lip of the last wing-feather
as it suddenly bursts into flame with sunlight
and starlight and, a dazzling pentecostal
tongue, plunges deep into the opposite horizon.
Stunned, our arms wrapped around each other in
a warmth of friendship, frost of fear, we walk
back into the house that hovers gently in the dark,
a familiar, ancient ship.
      And when we speak again,
softly, anxious as first lovers or as lovers who
have lived a lifetime when they go to bed, we will
not speak of another season's longing or of one
more and more inexorable migration, but we shall
speak about the garden to be sown, the brilliance
of the stars, this gift that makes our bodies ache.

III

A MOMENTARY

ORDER

A Nest of Sonnets

These harbingers of spring are really dumb.
Winter isn't over yet; the trees
aren't in full bloom; the weatherman still sees
a chance of frost; the worms are all quite numb
with their long sleep deep in the thawing ground.
But here is robin redbreast, hard at work
on this year's nest; the tomcat goes berserk;
a thin snow starts to fall without a sound.

These birds will risk their lives just to insist
on summer, sing until our bones turn green
and blossom into song, until our lean
but swelling tongues cry out: "Robin, desist!

Your wiser brothers send you on ahead
to find out whether we're alive or dead."

. . .

Now why does that forsythia insist
on masquerading as the burning bush?
Such beauty ought to know how to resist
that old temptation, know how not to rush

right in where even Moses never tread.
No wonder birds don't nest inside its limbs.
Their lives are tough enough; they've learned to dread
the law asserting beauty skims

the terror from the truth. The hares begin
to nibble at the fiery blooms. Too soon
the burning petals of that bush, at noon,
will fizzle, fall, the core of beauty's sin:

to worship galaxies of burnt-out stars
that never saved us from our lust and wars.

•　　•　　•

A woodsy drama is unfolding here:
the robin's hatching this year's brood; she flits
from hemlock to the lawn, where she just sits
and stares back at the sun till she can hear
a worm start stirring underfoot.

                              Nearby,
the chipmunk's silly with the smell of eggs;
he sniffs and skitters on his tiny legs
as if waltzing on blue shells.
                              The grackle, high
atop the pine, sits patiently and mute.
And while the robin makes the chipmunk scoot,
attacks him like a hawk or simply begs
him off, the grackle gobbles up the eggs.

Ah, redbreast, if your enemy can't kill
your babies, then your sister surely will.

•   •   •

The sound of copulation's in the air!
A bright red cardinal repeats his mate's
own blazing passion; and the robin baits
the robin with her warble. Here and there

the bees begin to pollinate the air,
their breathless hum the buzz of sperm, while doves
coo-coo the wiser notes of their long love's
refrain and young boys whistle everywhere

they go to chase the girls. We must beware
of so much propagation, so much song
in spring, remember winter nights are long
and poems fruitless to the heart's that bare.

Ah, Love, why hunt for rhymes, when everywhere
the sound of copulation's in the air!

•   •   •

I'm getting sick of all this tender rustic stuff
about the birds and bees, the robin on the wing.
It's autumn in my life; I know it isn't spring.
I think the time has come for someone to get rough.

A farmer's son, I haven't worked hard all my life
escaping from the farm in me, to come full cir-
cle back to plowing trusty mother nature. Sir,
there must be more to art and life than simply *life*.

I want to murder and create (perhaps a hit
on Broadway) characters on a much grander scale,
then live like royalty just off the sale.
I want to write an epic celebrating *shit*.

For stronger muses there is always tougher meat
than birds and bees and sonnets plodding on six feet.

•   •   •

The weatherman was right, of course: last night
a frost that threatened the forsythia,
our new tomato plants, and made plasma
in our tongues freeze at the pitch of fright,

our conversations elegies of loss.
It will take days to know what did survive,
what perished. Lord, up here we seem to thrive
because the loaded odds sift out the dross,

the timid and too frail. We can depend
on summer being just as long and fierce,
on sunlight that's so bitter it can pierce
you to the bone. Who knows how it will end.

The battle isn't over yet, redbreast:
the kiss of frost still lingers on your nest.

•　　•　　•

But look, while we were worrying to death
about our flowers' fate, our lettuce patch,
this bird did what she'd meant to do: just hatch
her eggs. Her babies throb with their first breath,

each heartbeat more astounding than the first.
And yet, though three chicks more than fill the nest,
there were four eggs. What tiny foetal test
condemned the fourth, what urgent bloody thirst

that could be satisfied with one blue egg?
But why should greater logic rule *their* lives?
In any sphere, what will survive, survives:
an armless man, a chicken with one leg.

These chicks can't fret their temporary plight,
when all their instincts concentrate on flight.

. . .

These moths won't settle for a simple death
like birds. They have to be theatrical,
like poets restless for ethereal
rewards so much they simply hold their breath.

So that one drowns in your last glass of scotch
or kamikazes your lit cigarettes;
another loiters as if taking bets
his fizzle will be brighter, he won't botch

his final exit. This one's wings are spread
into a white and delicate tutu;
then, when her beauty's captivated you,
she spins atop her head until she's dead.

I won't be conned by flashy suicide;
my dance with death will be one long, slow stride.

•　　•　　•

Well, Wildebeest, what do you think of that?
You stare at me as if you knew just one
small useless fact that might restore the fun
I lost to art. You silly household cat,

about this business you know less than I
do. You get your three meals a day on time
and you sleep mindlessly until the chime
awakens you in time to watch the sky

for birds that fly as soundless as a dream,
as bloodless. Just what did you do today
to earn your name as predator and prey,
to prove you aren't the neutered pet you seem?

Your speechless answer tumbles from your mouth:
another songbird that will not fly south.

●　　●　　●

What happened to the farmer's son in me
who'd feed or slaughter hens, a pig, a cow
with equal absences of care and now
debates the pattern of their *areté*

with zeal, as if his very soul's at stake?
There are these sleepless sharks that swim in all
creation swimming sleeplessly, its small
ferocious foetuses. Our great mistake

is to forget the song that mother-shark
sings softly as she swims: "Devour one
another, oh my babies; only one
of you will live to be a sleepless shark."

Where is the sleeping farmer's son in me
who reaps these sonnets of anxiety?

The Slaughter of Pigs

TO DAPHNE

We take our goblets of red dinner wine
into the living room, light
glass candles whose pale glow's scented with
the fragrance of fresh pine, and

we stretch out on the white wool rug, as if it
were an island beach that shelved
on some other time and place. From the heart
of arctic wastes that once shaped

this landscape we inhabit, a storm is
raging in another year.
We watch snowflakes disappear into
the gullet of a howling

wind, and I remind you of the time we
stood by another window
in another storm. Pointing to the flakes,
you softly sang: "Oh, Daddy, see,

they look like fishes diving into the ground!"
Daphne, tonight you're far more
fragile than you were years ago when
I first held you in my arms

ten minutes after birth, before you'd had
the time to be transformed from
some primal creature (the milky lunar
casing of the womb still clinging

to your flesh) into my daughter, into this
young woman who, with those wiles
you're just discovering you have, convinces
me to slaughter your pink pig.

Our living room becomes a barnyard; we
lay the pig down on its back;
you squeal as if you were a baby once
again; you offer me the knife.

       •   •   •

I slip the carving knife into your pig's
tough underside, guide the blade
up to its bloodless, silent throat as if
I had done this all my life . . .

and that high breathless wheeze, that childish
whine of frantic pigs rises
once again above clean pails of steaming
blood in Dingley's slaughter house.

Sledge hammers thud another snout; and when
its skin and bristles have been
tenderized in vats of boiling water,
its carcass pulleyed up, when

it hangs there in fall light, its hooves
dancing softly on the wooden floor,
its head thrown back in sheer abandonment
to hide some soundless promise

of revenge raging in its small blind eyes—
like the bloated body of
a pink and hairy criminal left on
the scaffold as an omen—

with the calm precision of a surgeon,
Dingley slits the pig's soft breast
and belly and leaps back, just as the rush
of viscera and bowels

fills a washtub, their sweet odor fills our
lungs, and vomit fills my mouth
again and then again. We load the tub,
the pails of blood, the carcass

on our pickup truck. Dingley wipes his brow,
waves a bloody hand and grins.
As we haul our load away, we hear sledge
hammers thud another snout.

•   •   •

Like a witness at an execution
your eyes flash wide with horror,
then with tender fascination. But I tell
you, Daphne, there's no pleasure

and no pity in this childhood story.
Such slaughter's just another
way of life. Hitler had invaded France;
our uncles wrote us from somewhere

in the Orient; Kamikaze dove
into our dreams; and Roosevelt
inspired us to greater and still greater
sacrifice, until every

simple human thing we did became
a total act of war and
this world a planetary charnel house.
We hoarded cans, glass, rubber bands

to be melted down and molded into
deadly weapons; blue-flowered
sacks of chicken-feed became my sister's
dresses and then rags to wash

the windows, floors; once a day we gathered
eggs; once a week, with an axe
in one hand and a squawking chicken in
another, my father walked

up to the tree stump out behind the barn
and in a simple, graceful
act, seemingly enlisting every
muscle in his body, he

chopped off the chicken's head, tossed the torso
down, still squawking, and waited
patiently while that decapitated
hen waltzed around him spinning

bright trapezoids of blood, until she
toppled long enough for him
to chop her legs off; and we played with them,
tugged the tendons that made those

scaly claws work: close, open, close, while Father
hunted through the entrails for
a soft-shelled egg, a gizzard and a liver.
At suppertime we listened

to the news on our kitchen radio, wrote
letters and wrapped packages
of chocolate bars and chewing gum for our
uncles, for our neighbor's son.

We wasted nothing. If we couldn't use
or eat or barter whatever
came into our lives, we shipped it to
the front to save another

life or waste it for our own life's sake.
And for our winter's table
far from battlegrounds, for our survival
and his own, Father slaughtered pigs.

·　　·　　·

But how we pampered them to death! For months we hunted new
tomatoes burnt by an unexpected frost or too much sun, sweet
ears of corn attacked by worms, and eggs too blood-speckled to
be sold or used.
　　　　　　We saved stove and table scraps, from seeds to
onion skins, leftovers from the plates of dogs and cats, stale breads
and pastries salvaged from the local bakery. We stirred them all
into barrels of buttermilk, milk we couldn't sell, milk we could do
without.

Sometimes it seemed that food was taken from our mouths just to fatten pigs for slaughter, as our days unfolded in a constant calendar of unquestioned rebirth and destruction, each human, animal and vegetable feeding off the other.

After supper dogs sniffed out the weasels and raccoons that came to graze in our cabbage patch at night. Cats hunted rats and field mice, trapping them before they ate the eggs we'd come to gather in the morning. If one hen was wounded and we didn't notice her, the other hens pecked at her wound, satisfying their own thirst for blood.

The cows chomped on the hay reaped from the fields where we had spread cow manure in the spring: we drank the sweet and foaming milk, still warm. And in fall we harvested a winter's store of vegetables from our garden fertilized by cow dung. What was taken from our mouths to feed the animals and earth, in time, returned into our mouths as food.

When pigs were slaughtered, the women also had to work even harder. Pigs were essential, long-lasting, worthy of the work. No part of the pig would go to waste if it could be made into some kind of winter fare in a symphony of old recipes that mothers sang as lullabies to their small breast-feeding daughters, near the kitchen stove, in the darkness of the long and lonely cycles of survival among those farming women.

Sometimes the work at slaughter-time killed one of us, while others simply died at war.

•   •   •

Too young for the First, just barely too old
for the Second, my father
never went to war and never taught me
how to hunt. When their fathers

bought them b-b guns and my friends shot
pigeons off the grange hall roof,
pretending those dumb birds that ate dry crumbs
out of our hands were Jap planes,

or later, when they went hunting with
their fathers, downed their first doe
or buck, skinned it, nailed the trophy of those
antlers on their fathers' barns

and, with manly pride glowing in their clouding
eyes, re-lived their hunting trip—
the stalking, silent waiting, every last
detail up to that breathless

moment when they stared deep into the eyes
of deer before pumping just one
slug into the heart of their stunned skulls,
filling those boys with release . . .

almost as much fun as jerking off when
you're alone at night in bed
or waking up in the middle of a good
wet dream—my father

said I wasn't old enough to play with
guns. He worked in the shipyard
every day, often overtime. And once
I borrowed Harold Dingley's

b-b gun. I shot at the grange hall
roof: all the pigeons fluttered
in a slow ascension of annoyance
and flew off toward the henhouse—

then one arced across the sky, across my
eye clouded by the blazing
sun, veered toward that small grove of pines
near the henhouse, just behind

the pigpen, suddenly collapsed as if
under the enormous weight
of its own life, and crashed through the branches
out of sight. When I found it

in a brilliant pool of bloodless sunlight,
its whole body throbbed with each
heartbeat, and the tiny eye at the center
of its head burned more fiercely

than the sun blaring overhead, the song
of cicadas ringing
like the ping of bullets ricocheting
in an amphitheater

of raw steel. For a moment lasting longer
than the memory of war,
I pumped pellet after pellet into
that bird's head, that ferocious sun, until

I caught my breath, until the sun, the eye,
the entire head was gone.
Daphne, my father never taught me how
to hunt. I taught myself to kill.

·　　·　　·

Where is my mother in this story? She
is alone in the kitchen
of our small upstairs apartment in
Grandpa Poulin's house and she

is singing, mending, she is baking; she
is lying on her back; her
muscles cramp and cervix welds and she
can't grunt or scream me out of her;

the fontanels of my own skull in her
refuse to fold and, as her
blood singes the low ceiling of her
bedroom, I'm ripped out of her

with forceps; the doctor drops me on her
bed, insists I'm dead, that she's
the only one to save; Aunt Marie, her
midwife, lifts and plunges me,

still blue and breathless, and baptizes me
in cold common water: *Je
te baptise au nom du Père, et du Fils,
et du Saint-Esprit.* And I

am born in blood and water. She and I
survived each other. Now she
is sewing, mending, baking still, and I
still hear the echo of her

voice sing out my father's name and mine, and I
sing back to her until I
come home for supper after dark, and we
rest, father, mother, me.

.   .   .

This winter storm is as relentless as
a father's memory. Plows
carve wide palpable circles of caution
around our house. Standing by

the window, I stare at the falling snow
as someone in a speeding
car believes he could be moving toward
the calmer center of a storm . . .

and I'm standing on the tip of that raft's
high diving board in
the middle of the pond, my whole body
addled by the height and dazzle

of refracted sunlight in the water
far below, a boy's senseless
ecstasy of being, of just being
this small boy with a new pale

dust of hair on my arms and legs, around
my groin, that ache at night
for reasons all their own. I take the deepest
breath I can, leap as high as

my will will carry me and, with my calves
stiffened, my feet kneaded to
a blunt point, plunge into the center
of the sun. Water opens,

a warm and total memory. Pliable
as lead, my muscles sink me
down until water thickens to a cool
and ancient slime, until

I'm buried to my waist in stirring
earth where uncreated
species sleep. I hover in that breathless
dream I've dreamed before, until

my ribcage starts to cave in with a wish
for gills, my arms frantic
to be fins. I must surface. My eyes open.
Above me, sunlight ripples,

a green and shimmering breath, so high
I'd open my mouth
for a hook. One more thrust of that small tail
contracting into legs, one

more shove of arms that grow against the odds,
their fingers webbed with water,
one more drop of breath breathed in another
world, trailing clouds of slime,

a molten skin emulsified by sun-
light, gasping for dear life,
my head tears the last membrane of water
into air that takes root

in my lungs again. My thin hair matted
to my skull, my face still blue,
I float slowly toward the rocking raft, haul
myself up, and lie on these

warm boards, exhausted as an enlisted
man after a day in boot
camp. This small pond in the woods of Maine is
my own training ground to test

how deeply I can plunge into this life,
how long I can last in that
other and survive to tell about them both.
I know the risks of going

and of coming back, but with my face turned
toward the blazing sun, I wait
until I'm prepared to climb this ladder,
to stand here on the tip of

this raft's high diving board, and, dizzy with
the mere possibility
of more being than any boy can know,
I leap again, and then again.

• • •

Like cracks in the glaze
of heirloom cups that
pass through the hands of
generation after
generation of
mothers and daughters,
none ever knowing
why or when that glaze
crazed and each staring
more deeply at those
lines than her mother,
as if into her
own palm or mirror,
as if holding her
face in her own hands
tracing the hard and
deep passage of days
that left their mark on
the topography
of her brain, diverged,
and all but the scars
they left have been long
forgotten until
now, when her days start
to converge again,
like tears in her veined
eyes, to be restored
into some kind of
whole that she can hold
in her cupped hands so
the scattered meaning
of her light might be
finally released
from porcelain on this
blinding summer day,

III

while her man's at war,
while her daughters are
asleep and their dreams
of lonely daughters
etch themselves in the
ivory of their skulls,
the blue of their blind
irises, as images
are scored on the rim
of memory and yield
no more meaning
than utter presence,
like cracks in the glaze
of this heirloom cup
about to shatter
in your hands and eyes.

      •   •   •

Coppers, nickels, silver dollars tumble
from the incision in your
plastic piggy-bank. The alloy of their
light sprays around the living

room, scars our faces, hands and thighs, steams
windows with the breath of our
high, shrill cries over so much metal
money it could fill a hogshead.

Daphne, we worked hard to fatten
your pink pig, saved every scrap
of change we had for years, sometimes just to
rob it back for lunch money

or for dinner at McDonald's when
we were all too spent to cook,
until it became so heavy, it threatened
to buckle under its own

weight, topple, crash down through the kitchen floor
into the cellar, its coins
squealing the amazement of such fall, like
the cries of young soldiers.

Your mother leaves her studio, craft and art,
steel fabrications of her
tongue, brilliant metal objects she will sell
to galleries and museums;

radiant with satisfaction, she comes
to join us as we toast in
another year we have survived without
the world at war, without sons,

brothers, strangers shedding blood in nameless
fields, women teaching daughters
the hard songs of survival in the dark
around the kitchen stove, men

hard at work in a necessary kill.
For the life of all of us
our fathers slaughtered pigs, our mothers
made that dead meat and blood

into our common daily food. Tonight,
as candlelight shimmers in
the residue of wine and the echo
of pine needles starts to fade

in this new year's dark, Daphne, my dear
daughter, we do what mothers,
fathers must do in another time and place.
We sing you other songs.

Begin Again

I

An aging migratory creature
    whose survival hinges on a yearly trek
        back to its species' native breeding grounds,

I have returned to this small coastal town
    in Maine where everything decays too soon
        and nothing ever dies quite soon enough.

Here, each day is another failure
    of another lifetime deposited across
        the foreign landscape of forgotten dreams.

Here, in the haze of oaks and elms ablaze
    with no more than a residue
        of oxygen and sap, cracked and peeling

plaster casts of dwarfed deer graze on blistered
    grass; whiter each day, winter brooding
        in their intricately beautiful and

brainless skulls, they inch toward old abandoned
    porches that will never be consoled,
        toward the char, the sudden frost, the utter

desolation at the heart of every
    open eye and palm. I was born here.
        My father's buried here, his father,

mother, and his brothers, all aligned
    precisely in the family plot according
        to the schema of our tree, and they root

themselves and me more deeply in this
    rocky ground than when we tried to work
        it for a living. Tonight I sit alone,

absorbing darkness resonating with
    the ancient music of the sea, the echo
        of our common womb, while far above that

distant, bare Atlantic field the faces
    of my family bloom, a brilliant tribal
        constellation ruling in a starless sky.

•   •   •

II

My wife and daughter are asleep, their bodies
 glowing with the sunlight they've absorbed all
  day, refracting their excess of light back

into the dark that barely touches them.
 Each day these two women grow into more
  beautiful reflections of each other,

as their limbs enclose the day's last rays
 of sun, petals of dark flowers that are
  still strangers in this motherland of memory.

I walk into the light of their deep sleep
 and breathe the nimbus of their dream:
  let these lovely women sleep; let them wake

refreshed; let them slowly stretch themselves
 open to the sun again, dawn clinging
  to their bodies' down, a brilliant dew;

and let them never get attached enough
 to this coastal land to long to live here
  as wild columbines flowering among the rocks.

Their history is unfolding in another
 land, a far more gentle future place
  where I may join them when my work is done.

Alone again, I inhale the dark,
 an ancient lover's breath: at last,
  tonight, brittle seeds of light begin

to orbit in my ankles, in my wrists,
 sail the uncharted inner space of bones,
  blossom with a meteoric fury in my mouth.

III

Like flocks of gulls around a fishing boat
  when the men are cleaning the day's catch,
    dumping heads and innards overboard, blood

blooming in the heaving sea, petals
  of ferocious underwater flowers,
    or as if my name were the intaglio

at the prehistoric center of
  each atom constituting their genetic
    molecules, tonight again moths swarm

at my window, perch on the precise,
  geometric lacing of the screen,
    a gleaming membrane separating

need from mere ambition, a film between
  blank memory and the future's incandescence.
    You know the myth of moths among the folk

here: they say they're souls of dead lovers,
  relatives and friends granted a reprieve
    from darkness one night every year to hunt

the living, offer you the secrets
  of the dead imprinted on their wings,
    flashing in their desperate eyes, in exchange

for particles of light swimming in your
  blood: glimpses of a future where the memory
    of sons is the fathers' fullness of desire.

And if you can decipher that rare code,
  they will hunt you down again next year.
    This is my fortieth. Those light-thirsty

angels have fished my veins a decade.
    I know more about the dead than I'll
        ever care to know: they cultivate

the mushrooms of their cryptic spores in
    the damp cellars of my chest where darkness
        rules and has been reigning far too long.

Knowing what was sown, what little ever
    flourished, what the fruit of that ambitious
        future surely is, finally the time

has come to cut myself off from a tree
    I never planted, to uproot myself
        from this unyielding land, to strip away

dead branches with those old nests and cocoons
    abandoned long ago, to set all that
        debris ablaze, and to begin again.

·   ·   ·

IV

The lamp erects a fence and stakes out
    a small pasture of pure light on the edge
        of one more day that would collapse beneath

the weight of so much darkness at its
    center. Wild with the very smell of light,
        a galaxy of moths—their wild faces as

familiar as my own, wings delicate
    and decorated, tiny heirloom doilies
        embroidered by a tribe of lonely women—

gather like a herd of famished deer
    after weeks of bitter winter, come
        to graze the orchard of my palms, gardens

of my two bare wrists. One by one I let
    them in, hold them in my outstretched hand
        with a cautious tenderness reserved

for the very fragile, the most precious
    of exotic flowers; one by one I speak
        their name with love, as if it were my own:

Alfred, Alphonse, Mélanie, Aurora,
    Azarie, Rose, Napoleon, Ovila, Émile,
        Florida, Evangeline, William, Laurier . . .

and one by one, in a measure of more
    light than they have ever known, without
        any compromise, for a moment that will

last them an eternity, they breathe,
    they rise, they suddenly disintegrate
        in the acetylene of my loving breath.

V

My table's littered with small stars of ash,
　　a burnt-out nebula that would never
　　　　fill the cupped hand of my sleeping daughter.

Before dawn breaks above the bay, before
　　my wife and daughter wake, never knowing
　　　　that the constellation of those ruling

planets rooted in the vast Atlantic sky
　　vanished as they slept, with my night's
　　　　work done, like a factory hand after one

more eight-hour shift, I wash the oil
　　and soot clinging to my hands and face and
　　　　stretch out in the glowing garden of our bed.

Dawn: a full and brilliant sun rises
　　from the sea, slowly hauling soundless
　　　　echoes of itself from deep within

our lungs, reverberating in our
　　open mouths and leaping from our lips,
　　　　as bright sonatas bloom inside our brains.

September 1, 1979

TO BASILIKE

Scientists have noted that over the centuries sharks
have been growing longer and thinner.

All day the bay has blazed a blue so blue
and so essential only to itself
it seemed about to surface and assume
a substance all its own. Shafts of sunlight

swam and darted through the tide, a school
of ancient sharks limned for sleepless centuries
by the sea, by instinct's will, and come
to our bay by choice where, one by one,

they made their final, everlasting leap
from fish to pure and elemental light.
Outside our bedroom window, mushrooms
have been growing blindly in the dark,

in the relentless rain of all-night storms
for days. Tonight they are a dozen suns
in orbit on the forest floor, their centers
palpable and orange August moons rising

from uncharted seas, spreading halos
of their spores around them on the intri-
cately delicate green face of moss, and
rooting in the sleepless blue still moored

in our eyes. If only for a moment
as deceptive as dead stars, on these rare
days we can believe we too are dreams
of this world that we feel slowly spinning

in its inner orbit toward what it dreams
to be. In our shadows lying at our feet,
the echoes of a hope we thought we had
abandoned long ago, our longings suddenly

ignite by instinct, mushroom into will,
fill us with a blinding glimpse of our own
rare and elemental selves leaping toward
that more essential, that more lasting

substance we must be, blazing like a pure
and newborn planet long before its light
is seen, shedding nebulas of bright
particles of dust rooting in the dead's

wide and sleep-blind eyes.
                                    Before I go to bed,
I raise the electro-magnetic mirrors of my hands
toward those stars where none of this earth's days
has reached its end, and I re-call today

before it dawns again, lightyears from now,
in a dimension other than our own.
As if to bless the cosmos for this one
day's glimpse and gift of what we are,

I kneel and gently cup my hands above
the calm and tender orbs of your closed eyes
still refracting light back into the dark
that barely touches them. My prayer, Love,

isn't to that void beyond the reach of sound.
Instead—before the winters dark descends,
before breath's tendrils turn to ice and
burgeon in our lungs, before crazed buds

of blood bloom and shatter in the barren
vineyard of our veins—my cupped hands brood
above your eyes until all energy is drained
from them, until your eyelids' luminescence

testifies: in you (and so in me) will dawn,
again and then again, this day when
all day the bay has blazed a blue so blue
and so essential to itself, to me and you,

that once, just once, we surfaced and assumed
this rare and elemental substance all our own.

〰   〰   〰

Saltimbanques

He was assailed by a sense of wonder for waste.
—DAPHNE ATHAS

I

Although summer's barely started, roses
are in bloom; you buy roses
for our small rented house, more red roses
than we have flower vases,
empty bottles for. And you laugh, "Roses
are for lovers!" Your flushed face
repeats and multiplies your lavish gift.

You stand in our villa's door,
ablaze, a reckless angel leaning
on no more than a scaffold
of sheer sunlight, exhaling oxygen
too rarefied for this heart
propped on the blood of others, reconstructed
to endure in that more common
realm where breath is forged into
brutal weapons in the mouths
of lovers. That gift of your love's
extraordinary architecture
would have been extravagant enough
to have sustained me for
at least one lifetime I have never lived.
But since you taught my body
how to love more than I knew it capable
of loving and survive, I
welcome this excess of roses, each bloom
excessive as a human
heart, as unwarranted as our love.

Two strangers magnetized
into each other's time and space by love's
stranger law of gravity,
we've learned the art of mastering the techniques
of our love's complicated
calculations taxing our bodies more
than the more fundamental
mathematics of the marriage bed.

And when we come together
at the pitch of our love's slow, agonized
amazement, every strand in
our tempered brains knows nothing will become
of us and nothing will come
of this love conceived as its own end
from the very start. For what
we do, we do for nothing other than
the simple act of loving,
of being nothing more than all we are,
all we've chosen to become—

just as a troupe of seasoned acrobats,
with no audience in sight,
will rehearse to conquer their contorted
limbs into such precise and
willed submission that in slow and total
unison all the bones
and muscles of their arms and legs, their ankles
and their wrists, begin to stretch,
to bend and arch, then bloom into a
more-than-human and amazing
flower, each limb a petal of the whole,
breathless and suspended in
nothing but the mid-air of imagination,
of the will to be no more

than just a flower of flesh that lives but
for a moment—seedless, issue-
less, glorious—and all too suddenly
or slowly sheds its all-
too-human petals of just ordinary
men and women back onto
the stage, back into the street, back into
the sidereal common
denominator of their separate lives.

3

See how those roses already
have begun to fade, as if exhausted
by the very will to bloom
trapped in their heartless seeds, which none has learned
to master, which still masters
them and spins them still atop their stems
to blossom once again far
above themselves, like an imagined corps
of high-wire saltimbanques
forever leaping, weightless, on the scaffold
of pure space. Our water will
prolong their death, the slow decomposition
of their perfect selves as one
more shape of what this earth has dreamed to be
in its decaying orbit
of the sun, calculated by the vast
imagination of millenia.
Soon they'll shed their petals, embers of
the tongues of memory burning
themselves out forever in their endless fall
back into the earth, the ground,
the forge of their imagined selves and ours.

❧   ❧   ❧

Husbands and Lovers

In my father's house late every
afternoon, the men gathered in
the stable, where Uncle Larry

sold them amber jiggers of rye
whiskey, bootlegging them at fifty
cents a shot. And while Ely,

sullen, shoveled cow manure,
they yelled at him, the only perks
of that small barnyard sinecure.

As whiskey burned their throats, they sat
on milking stools, on sacks of grain,
just fucking this and fucking that

as men do when they are alone.
They told stories, each new shot of
rye cutting closer to the bone:

Cliff Wallace tricking Chet Lachance
into buying a dead horse; Grace
Gould naked at the grange hall dance.

One time George Farrar paid his own
uncle to seduce his wife so
he could divorce her, he had grown

so sick of her. Larry's bastards
littering the beds of strangers'
wives and sweethearts . . . so many shards

of misbegotten seed. "D'ya hear
how Duke, the barber, got beat up
by sailors, that cock-sucking queer,

his dyed hair and white Cadillac!
Well, they found 'im, black and blue and
bloody, almost dead, in the back

seat of his car. I want to buy
my friend here one more drink before
. . . goddam, now I've forgotten why."

And if one pressed his luck a bit
to speak of what lay heavy on
his tongue, the others mumbled, "Shit!

Oh, shit!"—the white sound made by men
bred to be loveless all their lives,
lust flaring in them now and then

like coal-bin dust ignited by
the flint of foreign presences,
a lover's ghost, a shot of sky . . .

before they closed the stable door
behind them and drove off, not drunk,
just having died a little more.

• • •

What did they know of love, these men
who spent their days in spinning rooms
or in cleaning out a pigpen

for the sow to have her piglets
in, then devour all of them
but two that Larry raised as pets

on gruel behind the kitchen stove
until he slaughtered them for food?
These men, what did they know of love—

my small father and his brothers
who, when not working, mined their own
silent hearts for warmth in winters

and on summer nights, as they sat
in their dark living room, alone,
or on the front porch where they spat

out the phlegm of their decaying
lungs, laced with their heart's bitter blood
in moonlight, while butts of burning

cigarettes died in the gravel
drives like life-supporting planets,
their wives, the echoes of their threats . . .
these men who knew so much of hell?

        •   •   •

We sit at the kitchen table
in the comfort of the semi-
darkness, smoking, barely able

to unearth love's tongue we've buried
for so long in these root-cellars
of our hearts. We won't be hurried

by pent-up pressures of lost years
that have imploded on themselves
(we start and finish two more beers)

like the flaring star-tips of our
cigarettes burning themselves out
far inside our lungs. This hour

calls for what our fathers never
learned: the courage to speak simply
of our love of one another

as two men who have survived the char
of our fathers' love, and as
the husbands, fathers that we are,

instead of burning up our lives
in cellars, factories or stables,
and damning our sons and wives.

A Momentary Order

He's spent this long hot morning
in my neighbor's yard. Where weeds
were so thick their thin stalks hauled
growing clumps of earth along
both sides of walks and their roots
stretched the limits of the earth
in affirmation of what
would outlast cement—the will
of chaos at the heart of
a more primal energy—he
carved clean, wide, precisely-edged
and hosed-down paths gleaming toward
the center of a newer
and imagined world inside
the old. And he trimmed bushes:
spring's bright forsythias that
bloomed ecstasies of suns,
small galaxies of sharp and
yellow stars of burning sap
that swirled about themselves in
an orbit of fierce light and
threatened to become word, here,
in our backyard next to that
leaning fence—until the blooms
consumed themselves with the fire
of their breath, leaving small, black
open mouths in the tracery
of branches wild with photo-
synthesis; dark green cedars
that erected spheres of fragrance
shimmering above circles

of shorn limbs, pools of odor
all around themselves, around
him who released the geo-
metric symmetry of that
relentless upward thrust of
energy's green lava as
it vaults toward that dreamt-of cast
of form until the stunning
weight of its own shape plunges
it back down into itself,
only to leap up again
in ceaseless cycles of
impossibility, that
longer lasting harmony
of atoms at the center
of each cedar standing in
a long straight line between my
neighbor's driveway and my own.

After he had taken off
his shirt, brushed his blond hair from
his brow, held the hose high in
the air, sprayed cold scrims of water
on himself, and as his
body shuddered aureoles
of steam, he began to prune
the fruit trees. He clipped each twig
draining power into space,
stripped off tough ophidian
vines that twisted into tight
and tighter coils, imbedding
themselves in the bark until
in time the carcasses of
trees would be earth's monuments
to that bloody battle for

survival from the day a god
stood naked in the eye of dawn,
nameless in a nameless place,
and all creatures turned away
in shame, all but the two who
offered him their own nakedness,
the dim incarnate echo
of his voice reverberating
in them even after he
had recognized the pure light
of his beauty in the swirl
of atomic particles
in their muscle, bone and blood,
in the spinning nebulae
of eggs and sperm, the kelson
of his image, and he had
banished them to silence, cut
off from his breath by a sword
blazing like a cedar—and
was reverberating still
in this young man's body and
my own, as he stepped into
an oasis of green leaves,
absorbing this bright morning's light
to transform it into shade,
and gazed at the trees with such
satisfaction that small buds
of germinating fruit seemed
about to throb with a promise
in their pulp that had lain dormant

since that long-forgotten time
when clustered seeds inside their
core felt a naked presence
in the morning air, much like
the one that was stirring now,
there, among my neighbor's trees,
well beyond my reach and call.

Ambling toward his morning's
final task, the garden at
the center of my neighbor's
yard, his features had become
resplendent with abandonment—
a spray of light grounded in
the pool of hair above his
groin, surging in a single
jet of brilliance, fanning out
across his chest and pulsing
its reflection on his face,
a borealis of oblivion—
as if he wasn't just
a hired hand, as if he
wasn't simply cleaning up
a backyard left untended
far too long, as if he too
believed the myths and meta-
phors I was projecting on
him and his work, transforming
it into that more substantial
truth of art when all is still
epiphany, not sluggish
fact transmuted into act.

And I wanted to intrude.

I wanted to run out, storm
my neighbor's fence and shatter
the illusion of that once
pure, contained and human place
being recreated here, today,
in suburbia outside
Rochester, New York, reason
with him to abandon this
pursuit of some perfected
vision to reverse, right now,
the thrust of entropy at
the heart of all we are and
do—just beg this boy to go
and leave well enough alone.

We have long been civilized
by creature comforts and the
absences of hope that we've
sublimated into small,
neurotic habits of a
slow, diurnal suicide,
and we're vaguely reconciled
with living with the silence
of our sterile cedars' waste
of energy on dark and
interlocking limbs that block
our neighbors from our sight, with
our driveways and our walks all
overgrown with healthy weeds,
like ancient aqueducts that
moss has muted or the paths
in forgotten cemeteries
where once-harnessed chaos
has returned to brute chaos
catapulting toward that promised

peace ruling at the heart of
stasis, and with our lovely wives
whose love has hardened into
bristling tolerance of our
touch as we brush against each
other—two famished panthers
prowling in the desert—
and who, in a crumbling beam
of light on waning after-
noons while ice cubes calmly crack
in the spectral well of their
martinis, are lovelier
as they become momentary
memories of their former selves,
their bitterness released like
lunar blood, their eyes uncoiled
and closed upon a dream whose
dream stirs in our sleeping genes
entangled in the roots of
a silence that still blooms in
our dark mouths, cross-pollinates
each time we speak, and, in rhythm
with our breath, scatters seeds that
flourish like our own sullen
children which we raised in that
somber arboretum we
constructed (with the air and light
and moisture, the whole atmos-
phere scientifically
controlled) to guarantee
endurance, when that world within
our world we had imagined
and designed and labored to

erect—during those brilliant
mornings when our whole bodies
ached with a hum that threatened
to explode into static—
collapsed: like echoes of a word
uttered centuries ago
and imploding on the fire
at its core; like this language
fired to inhuman pitch,
sentences pronounced in vain
against the tyranny of
gravity and space; like
planets burning themselves out;
or just like that young worker's
construct in my neighbor's yard
and in my line of vision
might have crumbled all around
him (as he knelt and stared
into the flower garden
as if seeing multiple
reflections of himself) had I
simply closed my eyes, focused
on some business near at hand
and let him do the job that
he was being paid to do.

But, you see, already he's
begun to yank tall shafts of
wild grasses, panicles
of seeds hovering above
those corollas blooming in

the sprawling flowerbed; he
gathers faded ones and lays
them on his knees, gently,
as if once, even in this
life—last night, perhaps, as he
dreamed his own limbs were brilliant
petals of the cereus
unfolding into bloom,
a cup of moonlight glowing
in the desert night—he'd been
those flowers' unremembered
sister; off others he gleans
beetles as, in a desert
dawn and from the tips of thorns,
girls might pluck dew drops cautiously
with their translucent finger-
nails. He leans closer to the dark
and moisture of the earth at
the center of the flowerbed—
where the languid laboring
of snails goes on just as surely
as the loud parabolas of
bees humming loads of pollen
overhead, just as surely as
the orbits of wild planets
and their moons in uncharted
space, or atoms in the tip
of each hair that illumines his
worn body—and he fills his lungs
with the cool green breath of moss.

He uproots a few last clumps
of weeds; his morning's work is

done; satisfied, he smiles, while
outside his eye's periphery
unfolds that drama he has
yet to learn: to strip oneself
of memory, desire,
all ambition to achieve
that bold serenity in
the homicidal coupling
of the praying mantis who
decapitates her mate, even
as he fertilizes her.

With his bare back and chest re-
fracting as much sun as they've
absorbed, he has labored with
the patience of a man obsessed
with the meticulous details
of a vision that would change
the world. As if denying
our history, our species
and his own just by dint of
long, painstaking toil in bright
clouds of pollen he has raised,
its galaxy of micro-
scopic seeds clinging to his
body's salty, gentle sweat,
all morning he's imposed an-
other, momentary, but
perhaps more precious, order
on our all-too-resilient
and suburban wilderness.

He stretches in the total
shade of my catalpa tree,
he falls asleep and dreams, and

while the factory whistles blow,
while cicadas sing a high,
pure, unbroken ring of sound
around my neighbor's garden
and my own, suddenly the sun
this young man has absorbed all
morning long begins to rise,
to vault from his bare chest and,
in the center of his dream
in the center of my eye,
roots a blinding rib of light.

A. Poulin, Jr. was born in Lisbon, Maine, in 1938, of French-Canadian immigrant parents. He received a B.A. from St. Francis College (Maine), an M.A. from Loyola University (Chicago), and an M.F.A. from the University of Iowa. He has taught at each of the colleges and universities from which he received degrees, and at the University of Maryland (European Division, Germany), the University of New Hampshire, and the State University of New York, College at Brockport, where he is Professor of English and Faculty Exchange Scholar.

The recipient of grants from the National Endowment for the Arts for both Translation and Poetry, the Translation Center of Columbia University, The Research Foundation of the State University of New York, The New York Foundation for the Arts, and the Embassy of Canada, Mr. Poulin also has been Visiting Fulbright Lecturer in Contemporary American Poetry at the Universities of Athens and Thessalonika, Greece. His other activities include serving as a member of the Literature Panel for The New York State Council on the Arts, Founding Executive Director of The New York State Literary Center, Inc., and Founding Editor-Publisher of BOA Editions, Ltd.

Mr. Poulin currently resides in Brockport, New York, with the metalsmith and jeweler, Basilike Poulin, and their daughter, Daphne.

This book was designed by Tree Swenson.

Typesetting in Galliard

by G&S Typesetters, Inc.

Manufactured by Edwards Brothers